Written by Beatrice Fontanel
Illustrated by Anne Logvinoff

Specialist adviser:
Dr Jane Mainwaring,
The British Museum (Natural History)

ISBN 1 85103 054 9
First published 1988 in the United Kingdom by
Moonlight Publishing Ltd,
131 Kensington Church Street, London W8

POCKET • WORLDS

Big Cats
and
Little Cats

The cat curling up by the fire,
the lion on the prowl in Africa,
are part of the same big family . . .

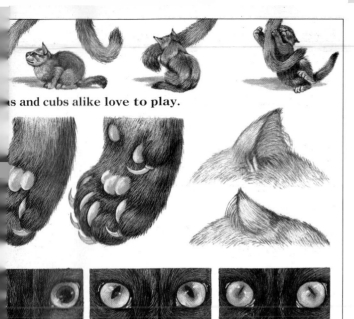

s and cubs alike love to play.

...lack circles in a cat's eyes let in light. In the daytime, the ...s close till they are narrow slits.

...e you noticed the whiskers on a cat's
...? If its whiskers touch the sides of a gap,
...t knows it's too narrow to get through.
...' noses are always damp. Particles from
...air cling to the wet, so that when the cat
...s its nose it can taste as well as smell
...t is going on around it.

Lions, tigers, cheetahs and leopards belong to the **family of felines.** Felines are mammals. When they have babies, the mothers suckle them on milk. All felines are also carnivorous, which means that they like eating meat.

Our most familiar felines are cats. Have you ever watched a cat? Look at it creeping carefully round a corner, on the alert for the slightest movement from mouse or bird . . . See how it sharpens its claws on a tree-trunk – or on the arm of a chair . . . Watch it waking up from a sleep, stretching out from ears to tail-tip, and setting off to hunt . . . If you scold a cat, it may sit down and lick its shoulder, sulking. When a young lion is put in its place by an older one, it licks its shoulder and sulks in just the same way. Cats may be pets, but they keep the habits of their wild cousins.

On the next two pages, you can see some of the cat's big relatives.

Made for hiding and hunting

Wild cats have different-coloure[d]
which help them to hide while th[ey]
stalking their prey. Leopards and
have dappled fur, tigers have stri[pes]
are all sorts of patterns, spots, st[ripes]
dappled markings, which help th[em]
merge into their surroundings, u[n]
unseen, until they are ready to p[ounce]
When a cat sees its prey, it crouc[hes]
its tail straight out behind, its ba[ck]
testing the ground with little twit[ching]
movements. Then, when it is perf[ectly]
balanced, it leaps forward like a[n]
spring. Its strong muscles and po[werful]
jaws mean it can kill animals twi[ce its]
size. Cats only kill what they nee[d]
Then they sleep or rest until the [next]
hunting trip.

◄ Black and brown dappled jaguars merge into
the South American jungle.

Skull of [...]
its strong [...]

Kitte[n]

The [...]
circl[...]

Ha[...]
fac[...]
a c[...]
Ca[...]
the[...]
lic[...]
wh[...]

Sometimes leopards may catch a monkey as it lies asleep in its nest in the tree-tops, but usually they hunt animals on the ground.

Cats prefer to hunt at dawn and dusk.

As the sun goes down, lions and lionesses stretch themselves and move out of the shade where they have been dozing during the heat of the day. After a drink at the river or waterhole, the lionesses set about the serious business of hunting. It is easier to hide in the gloom, and not so tiring to run when the air is cooler. Sometimes the lionesses don't make a kill, and the family, or pride, of lions have to make do with a carcass left over from the night before. If a pride has to change territories, it moves at night to avoid the heat of the African sun. A pride on the move can cover up to thirty kilometres in a night.

The flat-headed cat from South-east Asia feeds on

How do cats hunt?

Most cats are stalkers – they hide, crouched low behind trees or in tall grass, and creep up on their prey until they are close enough to bound out and leap on it. They won't waste energy chasing after an animal for long. They catch the young, the sick or the weak.

fish which it catches with its sharp claws.

When they attack, they knock their prey over. Then they bite the soft neck under the chin. With the cat's teeth gripping its throat, the prey quickly dies, unable to breathe. All cats like to eat their kill quietly, away from other predators which might try to take it from them. Leopards will drag it up into a tree, so that they can eat it at their leisure.

A leopard sometimes hides in a tree so that it can drop down on its unsuspecting prey.

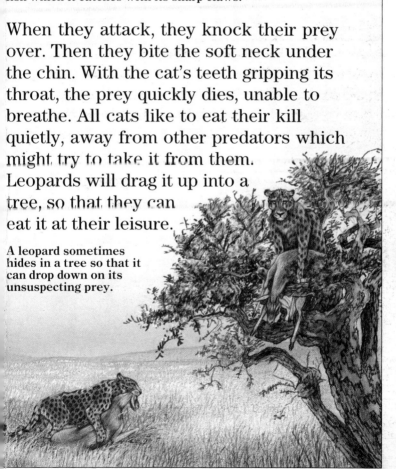

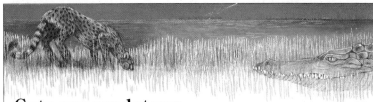

Cats are predators:

they hunt all sorts of animals. Leopards are as happy eating frogs as antelope. Cheetahs will eat gazelle and antelope, lionesses will catch zebra, gnu, and even young hippopotami.

Predators are useful

because they eat the animals which can't get away. The weak are weeded out so only the healthy animals survive and breed. Keeping down the numbers of grass-eating animals means that there is enough grass and leaves for everyone. Predators help keep nature in balance.

A giraffe discourages a hopeful young lioness.

But for all their strength and ferocity, cats have enemies too.

They are careful to avoid elephants, which may charge them and trample them to death, particularly if there are baby elephants to be protected. They watch out for crocodiles when they go to the water to drink, and for snakes which might spit poison at them or squeeze them to death. Young cubs find porcupines prickly playmates.

Lions live in a family group.

The pride is made up of two or three males, with their females and cubs. There may be twenty to thirty lions in a pride. Each member of the pride knows his or her place, with the dominant male in charge of them all. The females share the work of the pride, caring for the young and hunting. The cubs are looked after communally,

and will suckle from their mother or one of her sisters. When the sun starts to go down, the females set off hunting. They are not fast runners, so they hunt together, watching a herd to pick out an animal that is slower and weaker than the others. Then they surround it and creep up until they are close enough to attack.

Cheetahs are the fastest land animals in the world. They are built for speed, with small heads and rounded ears, flexible backs and long powerful back legs. They are the only cats without retractable claws. Instead, their claws act like the studs on a runner's shoes, gripping the ground and helping them to balance as they race along.

A cheetah can run at up to 100 kilometres an hour! But it can't keep up that sort of speed for more than a few seconds – if it hasn't caught its prey in the first 200 metres, it gives up the chase and drops panting into the grass until it gets its breath back and is ready to try again. Cheetahs hunt on their own. Because they can run so fast, they do not stalk their prey, but chase and catch some of the swiftest antelope that graze on the African plains.

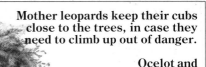
Mother leopards keep their cubs close to the trees, in case they need to climb up out of danger.

Ocelot and her young

How do the mother cats bring up their young?

Apart from lions, most cats are solitary animals, living on their own for most of the year. But the females share their lives with their young, teaching them until they are old enough to fend for themselves. While **leopard cubs** are young, their mother hides them while she goes off hunting. When she returns, she brings them meat which she chews up for them to eat. **A lioness** begins to teach her cubs to hunt when they are about four months old. She captures a small animal and then frees it near the cubs, so that they learn to chase and catch it.

Lion cubs feeding with their brothers, sisters and cousins

A mother leopard and her cub up a tree

Lynx cubs are born in a crack in a tree-trunk, or in a hollow under the roots of a tree. When they are two months old, they stop suckling milk from their mother and begin to hunt. In the autumn after they are born, they leave the family group and start to live on their own.

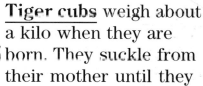
Caracal and her young

Tiger cubs weigh about a kilo when they are born. They suckle from their mother until they are about six months old. When they are about two years old, they gradually move further and further away from the family group.

Tiger cubs practise pouncing by jumping on their mother.

In Ancient Egypt, cats were sacred. When they died, they were made into mummies, just as the kings were.

Cats as pets

Dogs were the first animals to live with people. Hundreds of thousands of years ago, hunters found that dogs could help them track down game. Then people started to capture and keep pigs, cows and sheep. Having the animals close at hand, ready to use for food and clothing, saved the time and effort of hunting. Other animals were useful; horses, elephants and camels could be trained to carry goods and people. The very last animals to be domesticated were cats. They learned to live in partnership with people, catching rats and mice in return for food and warmth. On the next two pages, you can see some of the hundreds of kinds of cat kept as pets today.

A genet, the cat-like cousin of the mongoose ▶

◀ A wild cat: many small wild cats still lead a hidden, secret life away from people.

Angora

Turkish Angora

Main Coon

Persian

Peke-faced
Persian

Himalayan

Birman

Manx

Balinese

Somali

Abyssinian

American Wirehair

Chartreux

Cymric

Bobtail Scottish Fold Egyptian Mau Silver Tabby

Cream Short-hair

Burmese

Russian Blue

Foreign Lilac

Siamese

Oriental

Bombay

Ocicat

Rex

Sphinx

In prehistoric times, there were cats as big as cows, with teeth like swords: sabre-toothed tigers.

Their huge stabbing teeth were useful for slashing and tearing at their prey, making them lose blood and grow weak. But this way of killing was very slow. Another group of cats, the **biting cats**, proved much more successful. They killed quickly, with a powerful bite which gripped the neck of their prey. They are the ancestors of all the big cats and little cats in the world today.

Wildlife alert!

The snow leopard, the Bengal tiger, indeed almost all the big cats are in danger of dying out. They have been hunted for their beautiful fur until there may soon be none left in the wild.

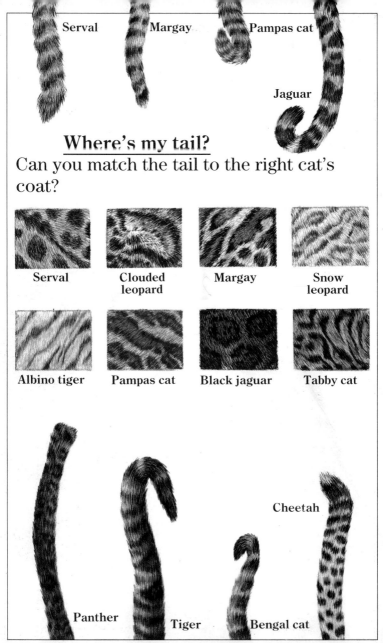

Serval Margay Pampas cat

Jaguar

Where's my tail?

Can you match the tail to the right cat's coat?

Serval

Clouded leopard

Margay

Snow leopard

Albino tiger

Pampas cat

Black jaguar

Tabby cat

Cheetah

Panther

Tiger

Bengal cat

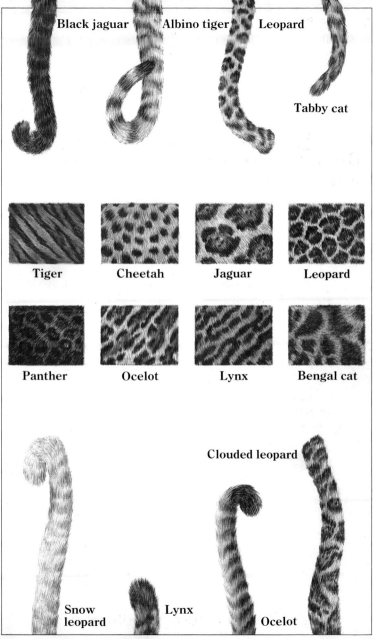

Black jaguar   Albino tiger   Leopard

Tabby cat

Tiger   Cheetah   Jaguar   Leopard

Panther   Ocelot   Lynx   Bengal cat

Clouded leopard

Snow leopard   Lynx   Ocelot

Index

Domestic cats

Abyssinian, 30
American Wirehair, 30
Angora, 30
Balinese, 30
Bengal, 34-35
Birman, 30
Bobtail, 31
Bombay, 31
Burmese, 31
Chartreux, 30
Cream Shorthair, 30
Cymric, 30
Egyptian Mau, 31
Foreign Lilac, 31
Himalayan, 30

Maine Coon, 30
Manx, 30
Ocicat, 31
Oriental, 31
Peke-faced Persian, 30
Persian, 30
Rex, 31
Russian Blue, 31
Scottish Fold, 31
Siamese, 31
Silver Tabby, 31
Somali, 30
Sphinx, 31
Tabby, 34-35
Turkish Angora, 30

Wild cats

albino tiger (Asia), 8, 34-35

black jaguar (North and South America), 8, 13, 34-35

bobcat (North America and Mexico), 8

caracal (Africa and Asia), 9, 27

cheetah (Africa and Asia), 7, 8, 20, 25, 34-35

clouded leopard (Asia), 9, 34-35

flat-headed cat (Asia), 18-19

genet (Africa), 29

jaguar (North and South America), 8, 13, 34-35

jaguarundi (North and South America), 9

leopard (Africa and Asia), 7-9, 17, 19-20, 26-27, 35

lion (Africa and India), 7, 9-11, 13, 17, 22-23, 26

lioness (Africa and India), 9, 17, 20, 22-23, 26

lynx (North America, Asia and Europe), 8, 13, 27, 35

margay (North and South America), 34

northern lynx (Europe), 8

ocelot (North and South America), 9, 35

pampas cat (South America), 34

panther (Africa and Asia), 9, 34-35

puma (North and South America), 8, 10-11

sabre-toothed tiger, (extinct), 33

serval (Africa), 9, 34

snow leopard (Asia), 9-11, 34-35

tiger (Asia), 7-8, 10-11, 13, 27, 34-35

wild cat, 29